SCHOLASTIC
News
Nonfiction Readers®

Our Earth
Saving Water

by Peggy Hock

Children's Press®
An Imprint of Scholastic Inc.
New York Toronto London Auckland Sydney
Mexico City New Delhi Hong Kong
Danbury, Connecticut

These content vocabulary word builders are for grades 1–2.

Content Adviser: Zoe Chafe, Research Associate, Worldwatch Institute, Washington, DC

Reading Consultant: Cecilia Minden-Cupp, PhD, Early Literacy Consultant and Author, Chapel Hill, North Carolina

Photographs © 2009: Alamy Images: 23 top right (Mike Abrahams), 19 (Rodolfo Arpia), 15, 21 bottom (Loretta Brennan), 21 top (foybles), 5 bottom right, 16 (Nick Hawkes), 21 center (JupiterImages/Thinkstock), 5 top left, 6 (Russ Merne), back cover, 11 (Nick Onken/UpperCut Images), 5 top right (Stock Connection Distribution), 5 bottom left, 9 (Jochen Tack), 17 (UpperCut Images), 2, 7 (Doug Wilson); Corbis Images: 23 top left (Yann Arthus-Bertrand), 4 top right, 12 right (Comstock), 20 top (Randy Faris), 23 bottom left (Michael Robinson/Beateworks); Digital Railroad/Bill Lies/California Stock Photo: 23 bottom right; Getty Images/Christopher Thomas: 13; iStockphoto/Tommy Maenhout: 20 bottom; Minden Pictures/Carr Clifton: 1, 4 bottom left, 10; PhotoEdit/David Young-Wolff: cover; VEER/Photodisc Photography: 4 bottom right, 12 left.

Book Design: Simonsays Design!
Book Production: The Design Lab

Library of Congress Cataloging-in-Publication Data
Hock, Peggy, 1948–
Saving water / By Peggy Hock.
   p. cm.—(Scholastic news nonfiction readers)
Includes bibliographical references and index.
ISBN-13: 978-0-531-13836-6 (lib. bdg.) 978-0-531-20436-8 (pbk.)
ISBN-10: 0-531-13836-4 (lib. bdg.) 0-531-20436-7 (pbk.)
1. Water-supply—Juvenile literature. I. Title. II. Series.
TD348.H63 2008
628.1—dc22   2007051899

CONTENTS

WORD HUNT

Look for these words as you read. They will be in **bold**.

drain
(drayn)

freshwater
(**fresh**-waw-tur)

gallons
(**ga**-luhnz)

Earth
(urth)

faucet
(**faw**-sit)

salt water
(sawlt **waw**-tur)

sprinkler
(**sprin**-klur)

5

Earth's Water

Can you imagine our world without water?

There would be no people. There would be no plants or animals either.

Living things on **Earth** need water.

Earth

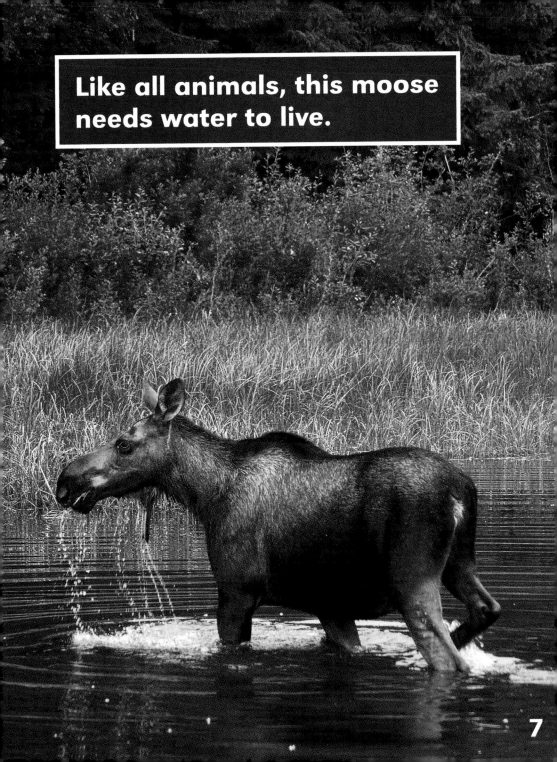

Like all animals, this moose needs water to live.

Did you know that most of Earth is covered with water? But most of that water is **salt water**.

Salt water is in the oceans.

It is not good to drink.

Only a little of Earth's water is water that people can use.

Ocean water isn't good for drinking, but it is good for swimming!

Water people can use is not salty. It is called **freshwater**.

People need freshwater for drinking, keeping clean, and growing food.

Freshwater is found in rivers, lakes, and under the ground.

freshwater

Rain and snow bring
freshwater to Earth.

Some families use about 400 **gallons** (1,514 liters) of freshwater each day. That's enough to fill more than 11 bathtubs!

Dirty water goes down the **drain** in toilets, sinks, and baths.

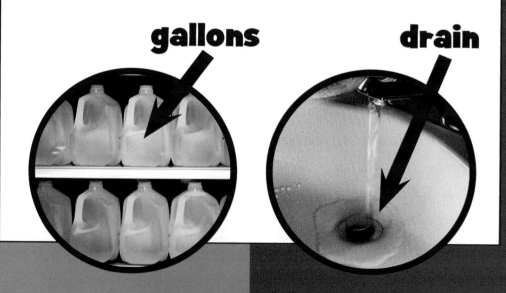

gallons

drain

You will save water if you take a quick shower instead of a bath.

Simple rules can help you use less freshwater.

Do you run the tap for a long time to get a glass of cold water?

Keep water in the refrigerator instead.

Do you have a leaky **faucet** in your house?

Close the faucet tighter, or ask an adult to fix it.

Even a slow drip will waste thousands of gallons of water each year.

Did you know that you can save water outside, too?

People use a lot of water to keep plants healthy. Often they use more than they need to.

Place **sprinklers** so they water plants, not sidewalks.

sprinkler

Save water by using a bucket to wash your car. Use water from the hose just for rinsing off the soap.

17

There are many more ways to save water.

If it looks like it's going to rain, don't water your garden. Let the rainwater do the work.

Think about the freshwater you use in your yard, your home, and your school.

Can you think of other ways to save some?

Freshwater is good for drinking, washing, and even playing!

Be a Water Detective

Look at these pictures.
Can you find five ways to save water?

1

2

5

4

3

Answers on page 24 **21**

YOUR NEW WORDS

drain (drayn) a pipe that takes away water

Earth (urth) the planet we live on

gallons (**ga**-luhnz) a liquid measurement; a gallon is equal to 4 quarts

faucet (**faw**-sit) an attachment to a pipe that lets water out

freshwater (**fresh**-waw-tur) water that is not salty. You use it for drinking, washing, and watering plants.

salt water (sawlt **waw**-tur) water that has salt in it. Water in the oceans is salt water. It is not good for drinking or watering plants.

sprinkler (**sprin**-klur) a tool that attaches to a hose and sprays water

WHERE DOES FRESHWATER COME FROM?

River

Well

Lake

Reservoir

INDEX

FIND OUT MORE
Book:
Nelson, Sara Elizabeth. *Let's Save Water.* Mankato, Minn:
Capstone Press, 2007.

Website:
Water Education Foundation: Water Kids
http://www.water-ed.org/kids.asp

MEET THE AUTHOR
Peggy Hock lives near San Francisco, California. She likes to go
backpacking near the Hetch Hetchy reservoir, which supplies
her city with water.

Be a Water Detective answers

1 Turn off the water while brushing your teeth.

2 Keep water in a pitcher in the refrigerator instead of letting water run until it gets cold.

3 Fix leaky faucets.

4 Turn off the hose and wash the car with water in a bucket.

5 Move sprinklers so they water only plants. Water early or late in the day when the sun is not strong.

Where does your water come from?
Water falls as rain or snow. Water
collects in rivers, lakes, and oceans.
Some of this water can be cleaned and
used for drinking.

People work to make sure Earth has
enough clean water. This book will tell
you how you can help.

children's press®
an imprint of
SCHOLASTIC
www.scholastic.com/librarypublishing

Guided Reading Level:	J
Word Count:	269
Decodability:	59%
Sight Words:	56

ISBN-13: 978-0-531-20436-8
ISBN-10: 0-531-20436-7

U.S. $6.95

90000

9 780531 204368